Our Wedding Journal

CELEBRATING THE MOST
MEMORABLE DAY OF OUR LIFE!

From America's Top Wedding Experts
Elizabeth & Alex Lluch
Authors of Over 30 Best-Selling Wedding Books

WS Publishing Group
San Diego, California

OUR WEDDING JOURNAL

By Elizabeth & Alex Lluch
America's Top Wedding Experts

Published by WS Publishing Group
San Diego, California 92119
© Copyright 2009 by WS Publishing Group

Design by:
Sarah Jang, WS Publishing Group

For Inquiries:
Log on to: www.WSPublishingGroup.com
E-mail: info@WSPublishingGroup.com

ISBN 13: 978-1-887169-91-2
Printed in China

Place photo
from the wedding
day here

OUR WEDDING DAY

DEDICATED TO BRIDES AND GROOMS EVERYWHERE.
MAY YOUR WEDDING DAY BE ONE OF THE HAPPIEST DAYS OF YOUR LIFE.

Contents

All About Us

"I love you not only for what you are,
but for what I am when I am with you."
- Elizabeth Barrett Browning

OUR FAMILY TREE

Bride's Side

Father.. Mother ....

Grandfather.. Grandfather...

Grandmother.. Grandmother..

Groom's Side

Father.. Mother ....

Grandfather.. Grandfather...

Grandmother.. Grandmother..

Notable Relatives Bride's Side

....

....

....

Notable Relatives Bride's Side

....

....

....

"Families are like fudge—mostly sweet with a few nuts." – Anonymous

Place photo
of significant
relatives here

NOTHING SAYS LOVE
LIKE FAMILY

ALL ABOUT HIM

Full name: ....

Birthday: ....

Hometown: ....

Height / Hair / Eyes: ....

Astrological sign: ....

Siblings: ....

Pets: ....

Hobbies: ....

....

3 words to describe him: ....

As a child, he wanted to be: ....

....

A quote that represents him: ....

....

Best quality: ....

Best feature: ....

"Life without love is like a tree without blossoms or fruit." – Kahlil Gibran

Place
childhood photo
of groom here

SNIPS AND SNAILS AND
PUPPY DOG TAILS

ALL ABOUT HER

Full name: ....

Birthday: ....

Hometown: ....

Height / Hair / Eyes: ....

Astrological sign: ....

Siblings: ....

Pets: ....

Hobbies:..

....

3 words to describe her: ....

As a child, she wanted to be:...

....

A quote that represents her: ....

....

Best quality:...

Best feature: ....

"At the touch of love, everyone becomes a poet." – Plato

Place photo
of bride before she
met her fiancé here

SUGAR AND SPICE AND
EVERYTHING NICE

HE'S THE ONE

His best feature: ....

His favorite things: ....

His dislikes: ....

Favorite book: ....

Favorite food: ....

Favorite flavor of ice cream: ....

Favorite pastime: ....

....

His dreams for the future: ....

....

....

....

His first thought when we met: ....

....

....

....

"Love is an irresistible desire to be irresistibly desired." – Robert Frost

Place photo of
groom as a
teenager or
adult here

THE HANDSOME GROOM

SHE'S THE ONE

Her best feature: ....

Her favorite things: ....

Her dislikes: ....

Favorite book: ....

Favorite food: ....

Favorite pastime: ....

Favorite flavor of ice cream: ....

Her dreams for the future: ....

....

....

....

Her first thought when we met: ....

....

....

....

....

"Being in love shows a person who he should be." – Anton Chekov

Place photo of
bride as a teenager
or adult here

THE BEAUTIFUL BRIDE

REFLECTIONS OF LOVE

Reflections on the development of your relationship ....

....

....

....

....

....

....

....

....

....

....

....

....

Date: ....

The Start of Love

"Love is friendship set to music."
- E. Joseph Crossman

LOVELY TO MEET YOU

How we first met:...

....

....

Where we met:...

....

....

The person or people who introduced us:...

....

Funny story about how we first met:...

....

....

First Impressions:

• Bride: ....

....

• Groom:...

....

*"Love is a butterfly, which when pursued, is just beyond your grasp, but if you sit down
quietly it may alight upon you." – Nathaniel Hawthorne*

Place photo
of you as an
early couple here

THE BEGINNING OF US

OUR FIRST DATE

Our first date was: ....
....
....

Where we went: ....
....
....

What we did: ....
....
....

Funniest memory from our first date: ....
....
....

On our first date, we felt: ....
....

How we said goodbye: ....
....

"Come with me and be my Love / And we will all the pleasures prove."
– Christopher Marlowe

Place memorabilia
from your first date
here

PERFECT NEW LOVE

GETTING TO KNOW YOU

Our first kiss:...
....

First movie we went to see:...
....

Our favorite couple to double-date with: ....

First time he sent flowers:..
....

First out-of-town getaway:..
....

First gifts we gave each other:..
....

Surprising thing we found out about each other

• Bride: ....
....

• Groom:..
....

"Love looks not with the eyes, but with the mind..."
- William Shakespeare, A Midsummer Night's Dream

Place photo
from your
courtship here

HEARTS WERE MEANT TO BE
WOOED AND WON

OUR MILESTONES

Our first holiday together: ....
....

Our first Christmas together: ....
....

Our first New Year's Eve together: ....
....

Describe the first time meeting the siblings:

• Bride: ....

• Groom: ....

Describe the first time meeting the best friends:

• Bride: ....

• Groom: ....

Describe the first time meeting the parents:

• Bride: ....

• Groom: ....

Another memorable milestone: ....

"Love does not consist in gazing at each other, but in looking outward
together in the same direction." - Antoine de Saint-Exupery

Place photo
from a holiday
or family
gathering here

TOGETHER WITH FAMILY
AND FRIENDS

SO HAPPY TOGETHER

Favorite restaurant:..

Favorite hangout: ....

Favorite pastime: ....

Favorite movie:..

Favorite TV show: ....

Favorite night spot: ....

Favorite party we attended:..

Favorite vacation: ....

Favorite memory from the first year:

• Bride: ....

....

• Groom:...

....

World events that happened during the first year:..

....

....

"And think not you can direct the course of love, for love,
if it finds you worthy, directs your course." - Kahlil Gibran

Place photo
from a get-togther
or vacation here

A PERFECT DAY

FALLING IN LOVE

Our song: ....

Nicknames we gave each other: ....

What we did to show affection: ....

The first time we said, "I love you": ....

....

....

How did you know this relationship was The One?:

• Bride: ....

....

• Groom: ....

....

Who did you tell?:

• Bride: ....

....

• Groom: ....

....

"If I had a flower for every time I thought of you, I could walk in my garden forever."
-Alfred Lord Tennyson

Place photo
that reminds you of
falling in love here

HEAD OVER HEELS

REFLECTIONS OF LOVE

Reflections on falling in love...

....

....

....

....

....

....

....

....

....

....

....

....

Date: ....

The Proposal

"Always the beautiful answer who
asks a more beautiful question." - ee cummings

POPPING THE QUESTION

Date: ....

Choosing the ring was: ....

....

....

The perfect place for a proposal: ....

....

....

How he asked: ....

....

....

What he said: ....

....

....

Right after he asked: ....

....

....

"Let us not love with words or tongue, but with actions and in truth." - 1 John 3:18

Place photo
from the day you
got engaged here

THE DAY OF OUR ENGAGEMENT

SHE SAID "YES"!

The first thing we did was: ....

....

....

....

....

First person we called: ....

How our parents reacted to the news:

• Bride: ....

....

• Groom: ....

....

What our best friends said:

• Bride: ....

....

• Groom: ....

....

"Doubt the stars are fire. Doubt the sun doth move. Doubt truth to be a liar.
But never doubt I love." - William Shakespeare

Place photo
from your
engagement here

WE'RE GETTING
MARRIED!

CELEBRATING OUR ENGAGEMENT

We celebrated as a couple by:...
....

Our engagement party was held on:...

Location: ....

The host/s:..

Special guests: ....
....

What we did: ....
....
....
....

Best memory from the party:...
....
....
....

Favorite gift we received:...

"There is no remedy for love but to love more." -Henry David Thoreau

Place photo
celebrating your
engagement here

CELEBRATING
WITH FRIENDS

REFLECTIONS OF LOVE

Reflections on the proposal ....

....

....

....

....

....

....

....

....

....

....

....

....

Date: ....

Our Wedding Plans

"Love doesn't make the world go round.
Love is what makes the ride worthwhile."
- Franklin P. Jones

WISHING, PLANNING, DREAMING

We wanted a wedding that would be: ....
....
....
....

We chose our wedding date because: ....
....
....
....

Our wedding location: ....

Describe the wedding site: ....
....
....
....

We loved our location because: ....
....
....

"Give all to love, obey thy heart." – Ralph Waldo Emerson

Place Save the
Date card or photo
of the wedding
location here

SAVE THE DATE!

YOU'RE INVITED!

Describe the invitations: ....

....

....

Choosing the stationery was: ....

....

Planning the guest list was: ....

....

How many guests were invited?

• Bride's side: ....

• Groom's side: ....

Our favorite people on the guest list: ....

....

The most random people on our guest list: ....

....

Our wedding wouldn't be the same without these guests: ....

....

"Life is to be fortified by many friendships.
To love and be loved is the greatest happiness of existence." – Sydney Smith

Place wedding
invitation here

OUR WEDDING INVITATION

MUCH TO DO

The theme we chose was: ....

Our colors: ....

We chose these colors because: ....

....

Our flowers: ....

The flowers were special because: ....

....

The bride's bouquet: ....

The cake tasting was: ....

Our favorite cakes were: ....

The cake we chose: ....

Menu options we considered: ....

....

The menu we picked: ....

....

Our wedding favors: ....

"In all of the wedding cake, hope is the sweetest of plums." - Douglas Jerrold

Place photo of
cake, dried flowers,
pictures from food
tasting here

MEMORIES OF PLANNING
OUR SPECIAL DAY

THE PERFECT DRESS

Who helped choose the wedding dress?: ....
....

Number of dresses I tried on: ....

Favorite designers: ....
....

I knew it was the perfect dress because: ....
....
....

Most memorable story from choosing dress: ....
....
....
....

Style and details of the dress: ....
....
....
....

"Love is a canvas furnished by nature and embroidered by imagination."
– Voltaire

Place photo
of wedding
dress here

MY WEDDING DRESS

LOVE IS IN THE DETAILS

My bridesmaids' dresses:...

....

Traditions we wanted to incorporate:..

....

How we made our wedding personal:...

....

Special songs on our wedding CD:...

....

Our photographer and why we chose him/her:..

....

Our videographer and why we chose him/her:..

....

Our wedding rings and why we chose them:...

....

The gifts we chose for one another and why:..

....

"Sit by me, my beloved, and listen to my heart; smile,
for your happiness is a symbol of our future" – Kahlil Gibran

Place picture
of wedding
rings here

MAKING IT MEMORABLE

A FEW SPECIAL PEOPLE

Maid of Honor:...................................... Relationship: ....

Bridesmaid: .... Relationship: ....

Bridesmaid: .... Relationship: ....

Bridesmaid: .... Relationship: ....

Bridesmaid: .... Relationship: ....

Bridesmaid: .... Relationship: ....

Best Man: .... Relationship: ....

Groomsman:...................................... Relationship: ....

Groomsman:...................................... Relationship: ....

Groomsman:...................................... Relationship: ....

Groomsman:...................................... Relationship: ....

Groomsman:...................................... Relationship: ....

The best thing about our wedding party:......................................

....

....

....

"I awoke this morning with devout thanksgiving for my friends,
the old and the new." – Ralph Waldo Emerson

Place photo
of wedding
party here

THE WEDDING PARTY

ALL'S FAIR IN LOVE AND WAR

Most fun part of planning our wedding: ....

....

The funniest thing that happened during planning: ....

....

Things we saw eye to eye on: ....

....

Toughest decision we had to make: ....

....

One thing we disagreed on: ....

....

Craziest part of planning the wedding: ....

....

How our in-laws participated: ....

....

People who helped us the most: ....

....

"Who travels for love finds a thousand miles not longer than one."
— Japanese proverb

Place photo
significant to
the wedding
planning here

LOOKING FORWARD
TO THE BIG DAY

REFLECTIONS OF LOVE

Reflections on the wedding-planning process..

....

....

....

....

....

....

....

....

....

....

....

....

Date: ....

Life's a Party

"Laugh as much as you breathe,
and love as long as you live." - Anonymous

THE BRIDAL SHOWER

Date, location & time: ....

Theme: ....

Hostess: ....

Fun games we played: ....

....

....

Who attended?: ....

....

....

Favorite memory from the bridal shower: ....

....

....

Favorite gifts: ....

....

....

One word to describe the shower: ....

"Who, being loved, is poor?" – Oscar Wilde

Place photo
from bridal
shower here

THE BRIDAL SHOWER

THE BACHELOR PARTY

Date, location & time: ....

What we did to celebrate:...

....

Friends that joined the festivities:...

....

....

....

Funniest moment: ....

....

....

....

The bachelor party was memorable because: ....

....

....

One word to describe the party:...

"But friendship is precious, not only in the shade, but in the sunshine of life..."
– Thomas Jefferson

Place photo
from bachelor
party here

THE BACHELOR PARTY

THE BACHELORETTE PARTY

Date, location & time: ....

What we did to celebrate:...

....

Friends that joined the festivities:...

....

....

....

Funniest moment: ....

....

....

....

The bachelorette party was memorable because:..

....

....

One word to describe the party:..

"Where there is love there is life." – Gandhi

Place photo
from bachelorette
party here

THE BACHELORETTE PARTY

OUR REHEARSAL DINNER

Date, location & time: ....

Family & friends who joined us: ....

....

....

....

The menu: ....

....

....

....

Special toasts: ....

....

....

....

Most memorable moments: ....

....

....

"Love is the greatest refreshment in life." – Pablo Picasso

Place photo
from rehearsal
dinner here

THE REHEARSAL DINNER

REFLECTIONS OF LOVE

Reflections on the pre-wedding events ....

....

....

....

....

....

....

....

....

....

....

....

....

Date: ....

Our Ceremony

"She walks in Beauty, like the night of cloudless climes and starry skies; And all that's best of dark and bright meet in her aspect and her eyes: Thus mellowed to that tender light which Heaven to gaudy day denies." - Lord Byron

THE BIG DAY

The night before the ceremony, we: ....
....
....

Getting dressed with my bridesmaids was: ....
....
....

Ceremony date, location & time:...
....
....

The weather was:...
....

Waiting to see each other, we felt:

• Bride: ....
....

• Groom:..
....

"I have spread my dreams beneath your feet;
tread softly because you tread on my dreams." – W.B. Yeats

Place photo
of bride getting
ready here

GETTING READY

HERE COMES THE BRIDE

Who walked the bride down the aisle?: ....

Groom's mother or father's advice: ....

....

Bride's mother or father's advice: ....

....

Our flower girl: ....

Our ring-bearer: ....

The bride's bouquet: ....

The bridesmaids' bouquets: ....

The groomsmen's boutonnieres: ....

Special guests: ....

....

....

Special moments from before the ceremony: ....

....

....

"To love someone deeply gives you strength.
Being loved by someone deeply gives you courage." – Lao Tzu

Place photo of
guests or wedding
aisles here

OUR WEDDING
CEREMONY

TWO BECOME ONE

First thought when I saw her coming down the aisle: ....
....

First thought when I saw him standing there:...
....

The music playing was: ....

The officiant: ....

Our vows:...
....
....
....
....
....

Our first kiss was: ....
....
....

"Love is, above all else, the gift of oneself." - Jean Anouilh

Place
photo of first
kiss here

OUR FIRST KISS

HAPPY DAY

Favorite readings: ....
....

People who spoke: ....
....

Most romantic moment: ....
....
....

Funniest moment: ....
....
....

Filling out the marriage certificate, we felt: ....
....
....

After the ceremony, we: ....
....
....

"If ever two were one, then surely we.
If ever man were loved by wife, then thee." – Anne Bradstreet

Place copy of
program or marriage
certificate here

HUSBAND AND WIFE

REFLECTIONS OF LOVE

Reflections on the ceremony ....

....

....

....

....

....

....

....

....

....

....

....

....

....

Date: ....

Our Reception

"Wherever you go, go with all your heart" - Confucious

WELCOME TO THE PARTY

Reception date & time:..

Location: ....

We chose this location because:..

....

We wanted our reception to be: ....

....

When we made our grand entrance, we thought:...

....

The mood at the reception was: ....

....

The music that was playing: ....

....

The flowers:...

The table decorations:...

Our favorite part of the décor was: ....

....

"...Sweetly sound the wedding bells." – Eliza Cook

Place photo
of reception room
or memorabilia
here

OUR BEAUTIFUL RECEPTION

RAISE A GLASS

Loved ones who gave toasts:...
....

What made us laugh: ....
....

What made us cry: ....
....

Favorite toast:...
....

The most surprising toast: ....
....

Words that touched us the most:..
....

Drink we toasted with:...
....

Special moments:...
....

"Let us celebrate the occasion with wine and sweet words." – Plautus

Place photo
from toasts or
copy of toast here

HEARTWARMING TOASTS

OUR WEDDING MENU

Starters: ....

....

First Course: ....

....

Main Course: ....

....

Dessert: ....

....

Wine, cocktails or bubbly: ....

....

Wedding cake: ....

....

Other treats: ....

....

What our guests thought about our menu: ....

....

"Your words are my food, your breath my wine. You are everything to me."
– Sarah Bernhardt

Place copy
of menu here

THE MENU

THE TRADITIONS

Religious or cultural traditions we practiced:..

....

....

"Something old":..

"Something new":...

"Something borrowed": ....

"Something blue": ....

The cake-cutting ceremony was: ....

....

For our first dance, we danced to:..

Bride danced with her father to: ....

Groom danced with his mother to: ....

Who caught the bouquet?: ....

Who caught the garter?:..

Something unique we did:...

....

"Heaven give you many, many merry days." – William Shakespeare

Place photo
of cake-cutting or
first dance here

SO HAPPY TOGETHER

SPECIAL WEDDING GIFTS

We registered at: ....

....

Gifts we gave our maid of honor/bridesmaids: ....

....

Gifts we gave our best man/groomsmen:..

....

Favorite gifts we received:..

....

....

Most touching gift: ....

Most unexpected gift!:..

Funniest gift:...

We got just what we wanted from: ....

Gift we will treasure forever: ....

....

....

"Love keeps out the cold better than a cloak." – Henry Wadsworth Longfellow

Place photo
of gifts here

LOVELY WEDDING GIFTS

CELEBRATING WITH FRIENDS AND FAMILY

Favorite songs played at our reception: ....

....

The guest with the best dance moves: ....

....,...

Most memorable moment from the reception: ....

....

Funniest memory from the reception: ....

....

Our friends made the reception fun by: ....

....

When did the reception wind down?: ....

....

Our guests saw us off by: ....

....

Our destination after the reception: ....

....

"Let us be grateful to people who make us happy; they are the charming gardeners who make our souls blossom." – Marcel Proust

Place photo
from the
reception here

OUR WEDDING
RECEPTION

REFLECTIONS OF LOVE

Reflections on the reception...

....

....

....

....

....

....

....

....

....

....

....

....

Date: ....

The Newlyweds

*"To get the full value of joy, you must
have someone to divide it with."* - Mark Twain

OUR HONEYMOON

Our honeymoon destination: ....
....

Why we chose this location: ....
....

Our goal for the honeymoon was: ....
....

Resort or hotel: ....
....

Our itinerary: ....
....

How we played: ....
....

How we relaxed: ....
....

When we told people we were newlyweds, they responded by: ....
....

"Laugh as much as you breathe and love as long as you live." – Anonymous

Place photo
of honeymoon
destination here

HONEYMOON

HAPPINESS

A PERFECT GETAWAY

We spent most of our time: ....

....

Most fun activity: ....

....

Favorite memory from the trip: ....

....

Most romantic moment: ....

....

What we loved about being newlyweds: ....

....

The one thing that couldn't have worked out better:...

....

A funny thing that happened:...

....

Our favorite people we met:...

....

"Life is not measured by the number of breaths we take, but by the number of moments that take our breath away." – Anonymous

Place photo
taken during
honeymoon here

MAGICAL HONEYMOON
MEMORIES

WE DREAM TOGETHER

First thing we did as newlyweds: ....
....

The first time it hit us that we were husband and wife: ....
....

Where we lived: ....
....

Favorite new thing we bought together: ....
....

Favorite part about being married: ....
....

Differences in our relationship now that we are married: ....
....

First piece of mail we received as husband and wife: ....
....

How we plan on celebrating our first anniversary: ....
....

"The best and most beautiful things in the world cannot be seen or even touched. They must
be felt with the heart." - Helen Keller

Place
photo of us as
newlyweds here

WELCOME TO
MARRIED LIFE

AND OUR LOVE JUST GROWS

Being married, we learned: ....

....

One thing I didn't know about you:

• Bride: ....

• Groom: ....

How we changed or grew: ....

....

Something that caught us by surprise: ....

....

Our plans for the future include: ....

....

A special trip we plan to take: ....

....

Every day, we are grateful for: ....

....

In 50 years, we imagine ourselves: ....

"Where we love is home, home that our feet may leave,
but not our hearts." – Oliver Wendell Holmes

Place photo
of us as a married
couple here

TOGETHER FOREVER

REFLECTIONS OF LOVE

Hopes and dreams for our marriage ....

....

....

....

....

....

....

....

....

....

....

....

....

....

Date: ....